LIFE DOESN'T FRIGHTEN ME AT ALL

poems compiled by

JOHN AGARD

*For Yansan, 15, who likes rap music, and for
Lesley, 15, who likes rap music too but had
to pass judgement on some of these poems.*

William Heinemann Limited
Michelin House,
81 Fulham Road,
London SW3 6RB

LONDON MELBOURNE AUCKLAND

First published in Great Britain 1989

ISBN 0 434 92523 3 (hardback)
ISBN 0 434 92525 X (paperback)

Photoset by Rowland Phototypesetting Ltd,
Bury St Edmunds, Suffolk
Printed in Great Britain
by St Edmundsbury Press Ltd,
Bury St Edmunds, Suffolk

CONTENTS

i n t r o d u c t i o n

MANY TEENAGERS still see poetry as something you study and the poet as removed from life. 'Mostly about dead leaves and frosted windows' – that's how one teenage girl in a comprehensive school once described poetry to me. I hope the poems in this book will help to remind you that a poet can be man or woman, black or white, old or young. Poets come from all sorts of cultures and are inspired by all sorts of things – from a tiny pimple to the big wide questions about life and death and unfairness.

One poet, for example, was into mathematics before turning to poetry. Another woman poet in the book has a karate black belt. Incidentally, more than one poet claims to have failed 'O' level English first time round. So poets come from all streams of life. Don't imagine the poet as shut away in an attic, waiting for inspiration beside a cup of tea.

I have included occasional pieces of personal information next to some poems, as well as 'Poetry Patter', because poets, like all human beings, have their times of tragedy as well as moments of small talk and humour. Too purist an attitude can weaken the blood of poet and anthologist. This anthology is intended for those teenagers with an allergy to poetry, but also for any of you who may be seized with that rare and undiagnosed compulsion to paste a favourite poem on the wall. I admit that the poets in this book may not necessarily know how to breakdance. But all the poets have at some time known an outbreak of pimples, breaking voice, etc., etc. I hope something in here will inspire you out there to break into poetry /to break lines according to the urgency of your feelings. It isn't 'uncool' to admit to liking poetry.

My thanks to Jonathan, Dolores and Bronac of the Poetry Library for their generous long-long-term loans; my thanks to my mother for all the typing; and most of all, my thanks to the poets.

JOHN AGARD

5

body talk

LO COLE

SPELL TO BANISH A PIMPLE

Get back pimple
get back to where you belong

Get back to never-never land
and I hope you stay there long

Get back pimple
get back to where you belong

How dare you take up residence
in the middle of my face

I never offered you a place
beside my dimple

Get back pimple
get back to where you belong

Get packing pimple
I banish you to outer space

If only life was that simple

JOHN AGARD
Guyana/UK

I WAKE UP

I wake up
I am not me
I am bodyless
I am weightless
I am legless
I am armless
I am in the sea of my mind
I am in the middle of my brain
I am afloat in a sea of nothing

It lasts for one flicker
of one eyelash

and then once again
I am my full heaviness
I am my full headedness
I am my full bodyness
Here.
Hallo.

MICHAEL ROSEN
UK

TOES

Toes are like fishes
Swimming about at the end of your feet,
Never a care in the world,
But to keep hanging on.

JULIE RIDD UK; written at 14

Backsides

Short ones, fat ones,
some in between.
Some soft and flabby,
others all shiny and clean.

When their owners are resting
they are placed upon a seat.
Some take up only three inches,
others over three feet.

Some stay in rhythm with the hips,
others hang to the ground.
Some are just about right,
but most make a dirty sound.

DEEPAK KALHA UK
written while a pupil at Lister Comprehensive School, London

a long overdue poem to my eyes

Poor brown slit eyes
You cause me so much pain
But for you, I would be
Totally invisible.

When young,
You filled with tears
At the slightest provocation.
When children teased,
It was because of you
They hated me.

In story books,
Her big blue eyes opened wide.
But you, you narrowed into slits.

Hard brown slit eyes
Echoes of the pain
You mirror back the world,
And I can see them all,
Drowning there.

Soft brown slit eyes
Windows of the Soul
I can see you staring back
Frank, open, lovely.

MEILING JIN
Guyana/UK
Meiling Jin has a black belt in karate

****

T h e   T o n g u e

The tongue was the very first instrument
when it was played it caused a lot of excitement

now it can be played good or bad
the sound can be bubbly or be sad

it has been known to tell the truth
then again the tongue can lie like a brute

if you lie with the tongue it will get you in a muddle
and you will get trouble on the double
nah bother trouble
when trouble nah trouble you

I use my tongue to project the truth
and I hope I can inspire the youth

I wish I can play drum bass and flute
then I could be a one-man group
but it sticks wid I night and day
most of the time you can hear it play
                    BUMBA BUMCHA
                    BUMBA BUMCHA

It can be polite and it can be rude
but what is unique
about this instrument
is that it can taste food

LEVI TAFARI Born Liverpool.   Parents: Jamaican

****

A FAT POEM

Fat is
as fat is
as fat is

Fat does
as fat thinks

Fat feels
as fat please

Fat believes

> Fat is to butter
> as milk is to cream
> fat is to sugar
> as pud is to steam

Fat is a dream
in times of lean

> fat is a darling
> a dumpling
> a squeeze
> fat is cuddles
> up a baby's sleeve
>
> and fat speaks for itself

GRACE NICHOLS Guyana/UK

THE BREATH OF DEATH
(the cigarette)

This cigarette of which i light
Crisp as death as dark as night
Its tacky smoke will stick to my guts
It makes the food i eat taste like cigarette butts

My breath smells like an ash tray
Cccccan i stop smoking fifteen a day

This cigarette defies my will,
Like my history, to survive

But still
I play with pure death
How long can i sustain life
I died with stale breath

And cancer laughs at my heart
Eats me away till i fall apart
Grabs my fingers and changes the colour
The smell that lingers is death brother

And cancer laughs again you will PAY
Can you stop smoking fifteen a day?

LEMN SISSAY
Black British

HEALTH FANATIC

JOHN COOPER CLARKE UK

around the block against the clock
tick tock tick tock tick tick tock
running out of breath running out of socks
rubber on the road flippety flop
non-skid agility chop chop
no time to hang about
work out health fanatic work out

the crack of dawn lifting weights
a tell-tale heart reverberates
high in polyunsaturates
low in polysaturates
a duke of edinburgh's award awaits
it's a man's life
he's a health fanatic so was his wife

a one-man war against decay
enjoys himself the hard way
allows himself a mars a day
how old am i what do i weigh
punch me there does it hurt no way
running on the spot don't get too hot
he's a health fanatic so was his wife

**KEMBI
POKEREU**
Papua
New Guinea

dolphins

****

a one-man war against decay
enjoys himself the hard way
allows himself a mars a day
how old am i what do i weigh
punch me there does it hurt no way
running on the spot don't get too hot
he's a health fanatic that's why not

running through the traffic jam taking in the lead
hyperactivity keeps him out of bed
deep down he'd like to kick it in the head
they'll regret it when they're dead
there's more to life than fun
he's a health fanatic he's got to run

beans greens and tangerines
and low cholesterol margarines
his limbs are loose his teeth are clean
he's a high octane fresh-air fiend
you've got to admit he's keen
what can you do but be impressed
he's a health fanatic give it a rest

shadow boxing punch the wall
one-a-side football
what's the score one all
could have been a copper too small
could have been a jockey too tall
knees up knees up head the ball
nervous energy makes him tick
he's a health fanatic he makes you sick.

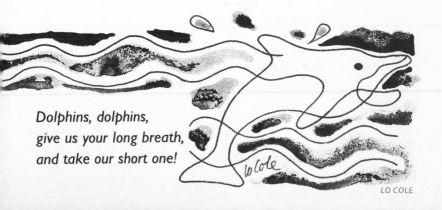

Dolphins, dolphins,
give us your long breath,
and take our short one!

LO COLE

****

T O U C H I N G

from *Songs for Nandu Bhende*

This is a song
about touch and touching.
You touch me – a way of feeling
I touch you – a way of understanding.
We are touched
by a film or a book.
We are touched
when a stranger is kind.
How can we live
without touching and being touched?

There is a healing touch,
it makes the sick whole again.
Let's keep in touch,
we say to a friend who's going away.
To have the right touch
means to know how it's done.
Touching is an art,
it's the movement
to and from the heart.

Some are easily touched.
Some are hard to touch.
You are often touched.
I am often touched.

NISSIM EZEKIEL India

Sweet sixteen

Well, you can't say
they didn't try.
Mamas never mentioned menses.
A nun screamed: You vulgar girl
don't say brassieres
say bracelets.
She pinned paper sleeves
onto our sleeveless dresses.
The preacher thundered:
Never go with a man alone
Never alone
and even if you're engaged
only passionless kisses.

At sixteen, Phoebe asked me:
Can it happen when you're in a dance hall
I mean, you know what,
getting preggers and all that, when
you're dancing?
I, sixteen, assured her
you could.

LUCINDA RODGERS

EUNICE DE SOUZA India

****

WHAT
THE
LITTLE
GIRL
DID

The littlegirl
   pulled up her bellyskin
      like a vest
         and examined her chest
            spleen, kidneys and the rest
               as a measled child a rash.

Sugar and spice
   and everything nice
      that's what littlegirls are made of

So she put in a hand
   and pulled out a gland
      and said: 'What a strange girl am I'

ROGER
MCGOUGH
UK

m u m   d a d   m e

TOMMY YAMAHA

I LOVE

I love me mother and me mother love me
We come so far from over the sea
We hear say de streets dem pave with gold
Sometime it hot sometime it cold

I love me mother and me mother love me
We try fi live in harmony
You might know her as Valerie
But to me she is my mammy

She shout at me daddy so loud sometime
She don't smoke weed and she don't drink wine
She always do the best she can
She work damn hard down inna England

She always sing some kinda song
She have big muscle and she very very strong
She like pussy cat and she like cashew nut
She don't bother with no if nor but

I love me mother and me mother love me
We come so far from over the sea,
We hear say de streets dem pave with gold
Sometime it hot sometime it cold

I love her and she love me too
And this is a love I know is true
I a-talk to you yeah you know who
Me and my mother we love you too.

BENJAMIN ZEPHANIAH
Born Jamaica, came to Birmingham aged 4

Heaven's in the
BASEMENT

Heaven's in the basement
I make my music there
I don't need a replacement
I spend all my days there

You can lock me in the basement
And throw away the key
I'll play my music
To satisfy me

The vicar's giving me a hard time
Because he lives next door
The people in the flat upstairs
Are banging on the floor

My girlfriend wants to know when
I'll take her to a show
But now I'm in the basement
I feel my music flow

Heaven's in the basement
My mum and dad don't agree
But I'm gonna play my music
To satisfy me.

MILES DAVIS LANDESMAN UK

father

My old father walks through
my heart
he never saved a thing his whole life
or put away
grain upon grain
or bought himself a house
or a gold watch
somehow the cup was never full

he lived
like a singing bird
from day to day
but
tell me can a minor
official live
long
like that?

My father walks through
my heart
in an old hat
whistling
happy songs
and believes with all his heart
he's going to heaven

TADEUSZ ROZEWICZ Poland

****

ANOTHER DAD

You're a fat old man
pleading for sympathy.

you huddle in the doorway
playing your instrument

badly – to embarrass me.
I'm your son, old man

I'm your son
and will continue to look

the other way
till you learn to play better

E. A. MARKHAM Montserrat/UK

****

Clothes

My mother keeps on telling me
When she was in her teens
She wore quite different clothes from mine
And hadn't heard of jeans,

T-shirts, no hats, and dresses that
Reach far above our knees.
I laughed at first and then I thought
One day my kids will tease

And scoff at what I'm wearing now.
What will their fashions be?
I'd give an awful lot to know,
To look ahead and see.

Girls dressed like girls perhaps more
And boys no longer half
Resembling us. Oh, what's in store
To make our children laugh?

ELIZABETH JENNINGS UK

TOMMY YAMAHA

YOUNg

A thousand doors ago
when I was a lonely kid
in a big house with four
garages and it was summer
as long as I could remember,
I lay on the lawn at night,
clover wrinkling under me
the wise stars bedding over me,
my mother's window a funnel
of yellow heat running out,
my father's window, half shut,
an eye where sleepers pass,
and the boards of the house
were smooth and white as wax
and probably a million leaves
sailed on their strange stalks
as the crickets ticked together
and I, in my brand new body,
which was not a woman's yet,
told the stars my questions
and thought God could really see
the heat and the painted light,
elbows, knees, dreams, goodnight.

ANNE SEXTON USA

mull

There is a boy here like me who catches fish
Big fish with their jaws all open
the villagers all wear wellingtons
and thin smiles and sometimes I wish

I was back home in Glasgow
because there only some people stare
this boy says we have the same hair
too – but I really don't think so.

Somebody asked if we are twins
but we aren't even the same size
I'm eight, he's only five
It's only 'cos we have the same skin.

My family's been coming here for years
I know this place like the back of my hand
yet still I feel this isn't my land
because of that look that some people wear.

JACKIE KAY
Black Scottish

Natural High

my mother is a
red
woman

she
gets high
on clean children

grows
common sense

injects
tales
with heroines

fumes
over dirty habits

hits the sky
on bad lines

crackling meteors

my mother
gets red
with the sun

JEAN BINTA BREEZE Jamaica

LUCINDA RODGERS

Me

I am me
you are you
I am nobody but me
you are nobody but you
I live for myself
I die for myself
You live for yourself
You die for yourself
You know I am me
and I know you are you.

**ACCABRE
HUNTLEY**
Born UK
of Guyanese parents

YOU & YOUR SELF

You
pleased with yourself
for freein yourself
havin seen yourself
in a world by yourself
not knowin yourself
to question yourself
about yourself
that enslaves
You.

MUTABARUKA
Jamaica

****

Hanging Fire

I am fourteen
and my skin has betrayed me
the boy I cannot live without
still sucks his thumb
in secret
how come my knees are
always so ashy
what if I die
before morning
and momma's in the bedroom
with the door closed.

I have to learn how to dance
in time for the next party
my room is too small for me
suppose I die before graduation
they will sing sad melodies
but finally
tell the truth about me
There is nothing I want to do
and too much
that has to be done
and momma's in the bedroom
with the door closed.

Nobody even stops to think
about my side of it
I should have been on Math Team
my marks were better than his
why do I have to be
the one
wearing braces
I have nothing to wear tomorrow
will I live long enough
to grow up
and momma's in the bedroom
with the door closed.

AUDRE LORDE Black American

Loneliness

My friends just left me
My family just walked out on me
My girlfriends run when they see me.

My enemies come up to me
Look after me and break my heart
When I walk on the streets the cars run
The lamp posts walk with me
But they do not say anything to me.

My property just seems to go
As for my life it is trying to walk too
But my body and senses go with it.
My bed even seems to move
That is why it threw me off last night
And I fell to the ground.

VIVIAN USHERWOOD Jamaica/UK
written at 12 at Hackney Downs School

CARMELLE HAYES

did jesus have a baby sister?

A SHORT NOTE ON SCHOOLGIRLS

Schoolgirls are heroes –
they have so many things to pass:
exams, notes in class, hockey balls –
and great big men on building sites
who go **WOOAR.**

ALISON CAMPBELL UK

****

HE MAN

Jumbo jets
never spit flame
like your fists

thump-a-man-a-day
keeps the world at bay

thump-a-man
never lets another man
overtake him

thump-a-man
never lets a man
push in the queue
before him

thump-a-man
keeps it together
knows what's what
and will thump
you if it's not what
for you too

thump-a-man
takes no shit, man

thump-a-man
will stand between
his woman and
the world
protect her
and fight her battles
for her

and if she won't
let him, then
he'll
thump her too

MICHELENE WANDOR UK

****

Antelope

A girl with legs like an antelope,
A boy with legs like an antelope,
Fell in love and got married
And had a pretty child
With legs like an antelope.
The child's father went away.
Where?
If you track the fast legs of an antelope
You need a faster heart.
Unfortunately in this world
There are very few hearts
As farsighted as
Antelope legs.

KAZUKO SHIRAISHI Japan

I LOVE YOU IT'S TRUE

I love you it's true but is there anything in that?
I loved baked potatoes and cheese,
Nice ripe red tomatoes and salad cream.
But does that mean anything?
Our tastes change and then infatuation . . .
Boredom sets in
And I must try something new.
But I love you and I loved Curly-Wurlys,
Mars bars and Fry's Turkish Delight.
Now my sweet tooth is dead.
I love you it's true but is there anything in that?

CAROLE STEWART
Black British

WHEN

When tigers don't roar
And beggars don't ask for more
When bums get off the street
and gamblers don't try to cheat

When football is no longer a sport
And there is no supreme court
When people sit on their heads
and in every pencil there is no lead

When no one in the world is true
And there are no animals in the zoo
The only thing that won't be new
are the feelings that I have in my heart
For you.

YANSAN AGARD Guyana/USA

LUCINDA RODGERS

DID

JESUS

HAVE

A

BABY

SISTER?

did jesus have a baby sister?
was she bitter?
was she sweet?
did she wind up in a convent?
did she end up on the street?
on the run?
on the stage?
did she dance?
did he have a sister?
a little baby sister?
did jesus have a sister?
did they give her a chance?

did he have a baby sister?
could she speak out
by and large?
or was she told by mother mary
ask your brother he's in charge
he's the chief
he's the whipped cream
on the cake
did he have a sister?
a little baby sister?
did jesus have a sister?
did they give her a break?

her brother's
birth announcement
was pretty big
pretty big
i guess
while she got precious
little notice
in the local press
her mother was the virgin
when she carried him
carried him
therein
if the little girl came later
then
was she conceived in sin?
and in sorrow?
and in shame?
did jesus have a sister?
what was her name?

did she long to be the saviour
saving everyone
she met?
and in private to her mirror
did she whisper
saviourette?
saviourwoman?
saviourperson?
save your breath!
did he have a sister?
did jesus have a sister?
was she there at his death?

and did she cry for mary's comfort
as she watched him
on the cross?
and was mary too despairing
ask your brother
he's the boss
he's the chief
he's the man
he's the show
did he have a sister?
a little baby sister?
did jesus have a sister?
doesn't anyone know?

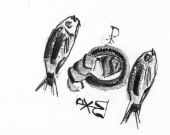

CARMELLE HAYES

DORY PREVIN USA

dis / illusion

Look at him, over there
Watch him turn his head and stare
I think he fancies me

See the way he turns around
See him look me up and down
I'm sure he fancies me

Look at his lovely jet black hair
I don't really like 'em fair
I just know he fancies me

He's coming over, ain't he great
He's gonna ask me for a date
I knew he fancied me

Hang on just a minute though
He's heading straight for my mate Flo
And I thought he fancied me

Ta-ra, Flo, I'll go on home
I suppose I really should have known
He didn't fancy me

I don't like un anyway
He's ugly
I don't fancy he

MAUREEN BURGE UK

****

Women Are Different

You dare not let your eyes meet theirs
for more than fifteen seconds.
Cos if you do,
You know what they're like
Liable to cross right over
to your side of the road,
and talk 'bout
'Daughter' and
'Sister' and
all that incestuous crap
You don't want to hear.
No,
You dare not let your eyes meet theirs.

However,
That's not to say that
Your gaze can't slide over
small, tight bums
And
Thighs carved so strong, and want to weep,
Or,
That real rude and stylish swagger,
Or hands that make you wonder
how they'd feel on those parts of your body.
Um hum!

It's just that,
You got to make sure that
they don't catch you out
When it's your turn to look,
Cos,
Then . . .
They'd know.

MARSHA PRESCOD Trinidad/UK

LO COLE

divorce

He would
in the case of a divorce
demand half
of everything
he said.
Half a sofa
half a television
half a summerhouse
half a pound of butter
half a child

The apartment was his
he said
because it was in his name.
The point was
that he loved her.

She loved someone
whose wife would
demand half
of everything.

That was in the marriage law.
It was as clear
as two and two are four.

****

The lawyer said
that it was right.

She smashed up half
of everything
and tore the tax sheet in pieces.
Then she went out
to the home for women on Jagtvej
with half a child

The child was teased at school
because he only had
one ear.
Otherwise life could be
put up with in that way
since it could not be
otherwise.

TOVE DITLEVSEN Denmark

T H E   M E R M A I D

A mermaid found a swimming lad,
Picked him for her own,
Pressed her body to his body,
Laughed, and plunging down
Forgot in cruel happiness
That even lovers drown.

W. B. YEATS
Ireland

LO COLE

Until The Next Time

I will put on
my overcoat
and tiptoe
through the ashes
of a love which took
so long
to die

And it is not my feet
you understand
but my arms
which feel the cold
Maybe in time
they will grow to know
the logic of my ways
and
still
these precious embers
    may melt my thoughts
    may warm my soul
    may keep me
in good stead
until
the next time

AMRYL JOHNSON Trinidad/UK

Mother's advice to the Bride after the wedding

Oh, child, behave like the tiger,
Behave like the tiger in the moonlight:
When it is dark, he bites.
Oh, child, behave like the tiger.
Your mother has behaved like the tiger,
She has behaved like the tiger in the moonlight.

Traditional:
East
African

LUCINDA RODGERS

telephone

I dial a number at random
and solitude

answers me.

**MAURICIO
VENEGAS**
Chile

loneliness

Who would believe that one could
be lonely and yet in love.

Loneliness is the blank sheet of paper.

KENDELL SMITH
St Kitts/UK

****

_B_EBE _B_ELINDA &

There was a girl who threw bananas about
When she couldn't get bananas she threw baseball bats about,
When she couldn't get baseball bats she threw big blue
    beehives about
And her name was Bebe, Bebe Belinda.

There was a boy who threw cuckoo clocks about
When he couldn't find cuckoo clocks he threw cucumbers about
When he couldn't find cucumbers he went crackers and threw
    christening cakes about
And his name was Carl, Carl Columbus.

CARL COLOMBUS

In Hanover Terrace, that magical place
Bebe and Carl met, face to red face.
She bust his cuckoo clock with a bunch of bananas.
In a swashbuckling sword fight his cucumber cutlass
    Carved her baseball bat to bits.
She bashed him on the bonce with her best blue beehive
But he craftily crowned her with a christening cake.

And they left it to me, old Lizzie Lush
To clean up the street with my scrubbing brush.

ADRIAN MITCHELL UK

Adrian Mitchell has expressed a wish for his poems not to be used for examination
purposes. But he doesn't mind them being read for enjoyment in the classroom.

TOMMY YAMAHA

flame and water

She steams him up
she makes him hot
she makes him rage
he boils over
he floods her
he extinguishes her

She regathers
she heats him
she makes him vapour
he regathers
he sprays her
he makes her smoulder

She regathers
she stings him steadily
she leaves him to cool
he regathers
he keeps up
steady drops on her flame

She warms him he wets her
She warms him he wets her
they carry on
and carry on
wishing for the secret
of balance.

JAMES BERRY
Jamaica/UK

propositions

TAMARA CAPELLERO

WHAT *HAPPENS*

It has happened
and it goes on happening
and will happen again
if nothing happens to stop it.

The innocent know nothing
because they are too innocent
and the guilty know nothing
because they are too guilty.

The poor do not notice
because they are too poor
and the rich do not notice
because they are too rich

The stupid shrug their shoulders
because they are too stupid
and the clever shrug their shoulders
because they are too clever

The young do not care
because they are too young
and the old do not care
because they are too old

That is why nothing happens
to stop it
and that is why it has happened
and goes on happening and will happen again

ERICH FRIED Austria/UK

propositions

I'm sad there's nothing to eat
the world doesn't give a damn about me
there shouldn't be any beggars
as I've been saying
year after year.

I propose that instead of butterflies
we put crabs in the gardens
— that would be better —
can you imagine a world without beggars?

I propose that we all become catholics
or communists or anything you say
it's a question of putting one word in the place of another
I propose we purify the water

by the authority vested in me by this beggar's staff
I propose that the pope grow a moustache

I am undone by hunger
I propose that somebody give me a sandwich
and then to have the monotony over with
I propose that the sun rise in the west.

NICANOR PARRA Chile
Nicanor Parra's first interest was mathematics and physics. In one poem
he makes a comparison between the poet and a bricklayer.

if my right hand

ZINZI MANDELA

written at the age of 12 Zinzi is the daughter of Nelson Mandela, whom she has seldom seen, because her father has been a political prisoner for the last twenty-six years in Robben Island, South Africa's maximum security jail.

If my right hand was white
and my left hand was black
they should meet only in prayer
because
they would not both be in one pocket
at the same time:
it would be too uncomfortable.
Why
do both exist on the same body
if it is painful
when they are together?

THE CAGE

SAVITRI HENSMAN
Born Sri Lanka 1962,
came to UK at age 2
written in the sixth
form at Highbury Hill
High School

The racist
Sweats to build a cage
For the black
Eagerly and urgently hammering in
Every bolt for every bar
While the cancer of fear and hate
Eats away at his heart
At last he looks round at his work
And gives a start
For the mighty cage is complete
And he, too, is inside.

TICKY

TICKY

TUCK

Ticky ticky tuck
everything stuck
Dem a look little wuk

MICHAEL SMITH
Jamaica
Michael Smith was
stoned to death
outside the Jamaican
Labour Party Office
in Stony Hill
on Wednesday
17th August 1983.
He was 29.

Wha yuh name?
Me no know
Whe yuh goin?
Nowhere
What yuh lookin?
Anything

Ticky ticky tuck
everybody bruck
What a luck

No wuk

dollar HORROR

de almighty dollar . . .
paralyse man like a stroke
harness man like a yoke
grip man throat till he choke
and still he end up broke . . . yuh feel is joke i
ah joke.

de almighty dollar . . .
more infectious than disease
it grip man balls and squeeze
bringing big big man to crawl on dey knees
in dey quest for financial ease

dis almighty dollar . . .
why de dollar man make
man take an make man slave
why de dollar man make
man take an send man to dey grave

****

why de dollar man make
man take an buy control
wid de dollar man make
man take an sell man soul
for de almighty dollar

an i done know already
dat plenty people go cry
on dat blessed day
when de almighty dollar
die
Amen.

BROTHER RESISTANCE Trinidad

A SONG FOR ENGLAND

An a so de rain a-fall
An a so de snow a-rain

An a so de fog a-fall
An a so de sun a-fail

An a so de seasons mix
An a so de bag-o-tricks

But a so me understan
De misery o de Englishman.

**ANDREW
SALKEY**
Jamaica

IF YOU THINK

If you think
Blows
Struck in Ireland
Won't hurt you
Think again
They will hurt you
If you think
The knife
Slid between the ribs of a Pakistani
Will glance off your lighter skin
Think again

If you think
Bullets hissing towards beating hearts
In some country we know nothing about
Will miss you
Think again
They will not miss your beating heart

If you think
Needles
Jabbed into veins
To make the blood run docile
Won't prick you
Think again

They will hurt you, hit you, prick you
And they will not miss you
We are all one
One trembling human flesh

LOTTE MOOS
UK

Lotte Moos had written the occasional piece, but it was not until she joined the Hackney Writers' Workshop at the age of 66 that she became a 'regular' poet. She says, 'There has been no time and place when *If You Think* didn't need writing.'

****

Objectivity

**MAHMOOD
JAMAL**
Pakistan/UK

**On a dark night
Only when you turn the light out
in your room
Can you see beyond
the window pane.**

ENLIGHTENMENT

is
sometimes
breathing
the street lamp
out
at dawn
and reading
between

**MICHAEL
HOROVITZ**
UK

the branches

THE WHEREFORE AND THE WHY

The Therefore and the Thereupon,
The Wherefore and the Why;
The Hitherto, the Witherto,
The Thus, the Thence, the Thy.

The Whysoever, Whereupon,
The Whatsoever, Whence;
The Hereinafter, Hereupon,
The Herebefore and Hence.

The Thereby and the Thereabouts,
The Thee, the Thou, the Thine;
I don't care for their whereabouts,
And they don't care for mine!

COLIN WEST UK

TOMMY IVIANNA

THE LESSON

Every time I'm called to the front
I answer every question
In a muddle.

– How are you getting on with History?
My teacher asks.
– Badly, very badly,
I've just made a lasting peace
With the Turks.

– What is the law of gravity?
– Wherever we find ourselves,
On water or on land,
On the ground or in the air,
Everything's bound to fall
Upon our heads.

– What stage of civilization
Have we reached?
– The era of rough stones,
Because the only polished one
Ever found,
The heart,
Has been lost.

– Can you draw the map of our highest hopes?
– Yes, with coloured balloons.
With each stronger gust
Another balloon flies.

From all this it's clear
I'll have to stay down a year,
And rightly so.

MARIN SORESCU
Romania

Marin Sorescu's poetry
readings attract such
vast crowds that they
have to be held
in football stadiums.

MATHS

What do you minus,
and from where?
I ask my teacher,
but he don't care.

Ten cubic metres
in square roots,
Or how many toes
go in nine boots?

Change ten decimals
to a fraction
Aaaaaaaaahhhhhhhhh!
is my reaction.

DEEPAK KALHA
UK
written while a pupil at Lister
Comprehensive School, London

EMMA CALDER

THE BUM

(Calypso)

Down dere in Stratford!

Me went down to dere
On a mission me did not fear:

To check out a certain myth:
Yu know it took a lat-a grit.

Me went to wake up Shakespeare,
'De deceased poet' of yester years.

Him ghost, dem tell me was down dere!

Dem seh dis great man passed away
Some time ago, Suh, because, me too
Want, to become great,
Me did want to ask am:
'A how him come suh?'

RAAS!

You know me see Shakespeare,
Drinking up stale beer,
Bumming around de town,
Picking up some crumbs,
Begging fu a dime,
Rhyming without time,
In dat ratten town,

You know Shakespeare was a bum!

JAMAL ALI Guyana/UK

****

A WISE TRIANGLE

Once upon a time there was a triangle
It had three sides
The fourth it hid
In its glowing centre

By day it would climb to its three vertices
And admire its centre
By night it would rest
In one of its three angles

At dawn it would watch its three sides
Turned into three glowing wheels
Disappear into the blue of no return

It would take out its fourth side
Kiss it break it three times
And hide it once more in its former place

And again it had three sides

And again by day it would climb
To its three vertices
And admire its centre
And by night it would rest
In one of its three angles

VASKO POPA Yugoslavia

insec' lesson

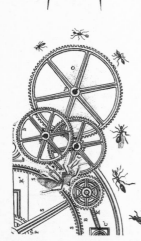

Todder nite mi a watch one programme,
Yuh did watch it too, Miss Vie?
De one wid de whole heap o' ants an' bug,
Mi couldn' believe mi eye

When mi see ow de ants dem lib
An hep out one anedda,
So much hundred tousan ants
Dey wuk an' pull togedda.

De momma ants she big an fat
So she liddung lay egg all day.
De solja ants tan up guard de door,
Mek sure no enemy no come dem way.

De worka ants a de bessis one,
Dem always wuk togedda
Fi feed de queen, an store de eggs,
An wash dem likkle bredda.

Some go out fi gadda food
Fi feed dose in de nes'
Some a dig hole fi mek new room
An some clean up de mess.

I' please mi fe see ow de ants dem pull,
An try fi get tings done,
Dem wuk an eat an sleep togedda
An a not even dem one.

Far mi see whole heap o' odda insect
Wasp, bug an fly an bee,
All a wuk togedda,
Ina perfec' harmony.

Dat couldn' happen a fi mi yahd,
Ivy woulda nebba wash Tim,
An Joe would mus dead fi hungry
If a Amos fi fine food fi 'im.

But uman-been fool-fool yuh know,
Look ow wi fight an cuss,
Steada wi lib in unity like de ants,
Wi lib like dawg an puss.

De man sey because o' unity
Mek de ants dem still around.
If we no unite, animals might soon start reign
Wid mankind six feet underground'.

VALERIE BLOOM Jamaica

blue whale knowledge

now the blue whale tells me
the earth is very sick
the blue whale knows
it swims oceans and oceans
and communicates with friends
300 miles away
by singing
avant-garde music
which I wish I had listened to more
but it had to be drummed into me
like I was a boy-seed
in a blue egg.

ZOLAN QUOBBLE
(Christopher Cardale) UK

THE TEACHER

MIROSLAV HOLUB
Czechoslovakia
A leading scientist,
Miroslav Holub
did not write
poetry until
he started
clinical research
at the
age of 30.

The earth rotates,
            says the young pupil
Not so, the earth rotates,
            says the teacher.

The hills are turning green,
            says the young pupil.
Not so, the hills are turning green,
            says the teacher.

Twice two is four,
            says the young pupil.
Not so, twice two is four,
            the teacher corrects him.

Because the teacher knows best.

THE SUN WITNESS

*Long ago a young girl
wearing a saffron coloured saree
walked gracefully
on her way –
She moved the square stone
from the white
near-dead grass.
By the lightening speed
of her black hand.*

*Silently, with her gaze,
she commanded the sun
to send its light
down upon everything,
even the white grass.*

*The sun accepted
her easy command
and came down with humility.*

*Days after,
she passed beggars in the street,
and tucked in her silk saree
to avoid their stains.*

*Seeing this,
The sun hid behind clouds,
and rain came,
unexpectedly, like tears.*

LUCINDA RODGERS

NURUNNESSA CHOUDHURRY Bangladesh

checking out me history

Dem tell me
Dem tell me
Wha dem want fo tell me

Bandage up me eye with me own history
Blind me to me own identity

Dem tell me bout 1066 and all dat
Dem tell me bout Dick Whittington and he cat
But Toussaint L'Ouverture
no dem never tell me bout dat

Toussaint
a slave
with vision
lick back
Napoleon
battalion
and first Black

Toussaint L'Ouverture
Rarely mentioned in school history books. A slave who led an army that defeated forces sent by Napoleon.

Republic born
Toussaint de thorn
to de French
Toussaint de beacon
of de Haitian Revolution

Dem tell me bout de man who discover de balloon
and de cow who jump over de moon

Dem tell me bout de dish run away with de spoon
but dem never tell me bout **Nanny de maroon**

Nanny
see-far woman
of mountain dream
fire-woman struggle
hopeful stream
to freedom river

> Nanny
> *A national heroine of Jamaica. She led runaway slaves to establish a free colony in the hills of Jamaica.*

Dem tell me bout Lord Nelson and Waterloo
but dem never tell me bout **Shaka de great Zulu**
Dem tell me bout Columbus and 1492
but what happen to de **Caribs** and de **Arawaks** too

> Caribs
> *Amerindian tribe from whom the Caribbean got its name.*

Dem tell me bout Florence Nightingale and she lamp
and how Robin Hood used to camp
Dem tell me bout old King Cole was a merry ole soul
but dem never tell me bout **Mary Seacole**

From Jamaica
she travel far
to the Crimean War
she volunteer to go
and even when de British said no
she still brave the Russian snow
a healing star
among the wounded
a yellow sunrise
to the dying

> Mary Seacole
> *The Jamaican nurse who put her skills to use in the Crimean War (1853–6) but who did not receive the acclaim that Florence Nightingale did.*

Dem tell me
Dem tell me wha dem want fo tell me
By now I checking out me own history
I carving out me identity.

JOHN AGARD Guyana/UK

My Little Boy

My little boy speaks
with an accent.
I must remember sometime
to lean my head down
and whisper in his ear
and ask him the name
of the country
he comes from.
I like his accent.

HENRY DUMAS

Black American
Henry Dumas
was shot to
death by a
policeman in a
New York subway
on March 23, 1968,
at the
age of 34.

I n q u i s i t i v e n e s s

Please, how does one spell definite?
Has it a double f in it?

Please, how old was Euripides?
And where are the Antipodes?

Please, what is a delphinium?
And whence comes aluminium?

Please, where does one find phosphorus?
And how big is the Bosporus?

Please, why are you so furious?
Do tell me, I'm so curious!

COLIN WEST UK

B Y E S

it's sad when a person gets off the bus
and looks at the one who stayed on top to wave bye
and for the one on top to be looking elsewhere

it's sad when a person gets off the bus
and doesn't look at the one who stayed on top waving bye
and walks off looking as though miles away

it's great when a person gets off the bus
and peeps at the one who stayed on top
to wave bye
and the one on top peeps down
at the one going along the pavement miles away but half peeping
and they both discover each other and wave bye

it's a bore when a person gets off the bus
and waves bye bye to the one on top who
waves bye bye

are there other possible variations?
(do this for homework)

MAURICIO REDOLES Chile

PHOTOGRAPH OF MANAGUA

From *Nicaragua Libre*

The man is not cute.
The man is not ugly.
The man is teaching himself
to read.
He sits in a kitchen chair
under a banana tree.
He holds the newspaper.
He tracks each word with a finger
and opens his mouth to the sound.
Next to the chair the old VZ rifle
leans at the ready.
His wife chases a baby pig with a homemade
broom and then she chases her daughter running
behind the baby pig.
His neighbor washes up with water from the barrel
after work.
The dirt floor of his house has been swept.
The dirt around the chair where he sits
has been swept.
He has swept the dirt twice.
The dirt is clean.
The dirt is his dirt.
The man is not cute.
The man is not ugly.
The man is teaching himself
to read.

JUNE JORDAN Black American

S O U R C E

Earth rounded
earthwise
earth held and contained
earth rooted

Spirit of air
come to me
blow me
thistledown lightly

Words can be flames
burning down to the source
words can burn
fire inspire

Oceans, seas
rivers, streams
lakes, pools
essence of water
bathe and cleanse me

MARY LEVIEN UK

DIRECTION

I was directed by my grandfather

To the East,

    so I might have the power of the bear;

To the South,

    so I might have the courage of the eagle;

To the West,

    so I might have the wisdom of the owl;

To the North,

    so I might have the craftiness of the fox;

To the Earth,

    so I might receive her fruit;

To the Sky,

    so I might lead a life of innocence.

ALONZO LOPEZ North American Indian

Don't do it my way

Do it this way do it your way
If you're looking for a sure way
Do it her way do it their way
Try the hip way or the square way
Leave it open leave it shut
Follow any passion but
Don't do it my way

Do it that way do it some way
You can make it any dumb way
There are problems and solutions
(Also mental institutions)
Play it hot or play it cool
If you want to play the fool
Then do it my way

****

We saw eye to eye
We always got along
You agreed with me
And we were always wrong
So baby

Try to make it on the highway
Or the safe way or the sly way
Try the castles in the sky way
Or the honest do-or-die way
But you never will succeed
If you follow where I lead
Everyone will say you blew it
If you're dumb enough to do it
My way
Don't do it my way

FRAN LANDESMAN USA

I KEPT ON PAST

i kept on past
the house where death was rampant
the house where death was rampant
the house where death was rampant

i didn't name it
not cancer it
wasn't consumption

i kept going

i kept on past
the street where death was dancing
the street where death was dancing
the street where death was dancing

it was skipping
it was stretching
it was beckoning
welcome

i kept going

i kept on past
the town where death was drunken
the town where death was drunken
the town where death was drunken

i had no friends there
that i knew of

i kept going

i was hungry
i was alone

ahead was the land
where death was king,
and the folk rebellious

AONGHAS MACNEACAIL Scotland

WE REAL COOL

THE POOL PLAYERS
SEVEN AT THE GOLDEN SHOVEL

We real cool. We
Left school. We

Lurk late. We
Strike straight. We

Sing sin. We
Thin gin. We

Jazz June. We
Die soon.

GWENDOLYN BROOKS

Black American

LO COLE

Break Dance

I'm going to break dance
turn rippling glass
stretch my muscles
to the bass

Whoo!

I'm going to break/dance
I'm going to rip it
and jerk it
and take it apart

I'm going to chop it
and move it
and groove it

Ooooh I'm going to ooze it
electric boogaloo
electric boogaloo
across your floor

I'm going to break/dance
watch my ass
take the shine
off your laugh

Whoo!

I'm going to dip it
and spin it
let my spine twist it
I'm going to shift it
and stride it
let my mind glide it

Then I'm going to ease it
ease it
and bring it all home
all home
          believing in the beat
          believing in the beat
          of myself

GRACE NICHOLS Guyana/UK

LO COLE

Green Velvet Suit

She was on the tube
I got on at Charing Cross
And like everyday
She didn't look at me
I even had a Green Velvet Suit
And a yellow bow tie
To make myself even more noticed
I dyed my hair really red

And I hope tomorrow
She will give me a glance
It's my very last chance
For the long week-end

ALVARO Chile
Alvaro is known as 'The Chilean with the Singing Nose', because he plays
the traditional nose flute.

A DRUNKEN EGOTIST

Morning sun
Ticking clock
Dirty cups
Musty room
Ringing 'phone
Stale milk bottles
like a stale mouth.

Sunday Observer
Sunday Times
Bacon and egg
tea and toast

Walk in the park
Man on the platform
Woman on a bench
Evening in bar
Drink in his glass
Swivering head
Struggling on stairs
Falling in bath
Falling on bed.

EDDIE LINDEN Scotland

Electric Avenue

Now in the streets there is violence
An-na-na lots of work to be done
No place to hang all our washing
I can't blame it all on the sun

Oh no we're gonna rock down to electric avenue
And then we'll take it higher
Oh we gonna rock down to electric avenue
And then we'll take it higher

Working so hard like a soldier
Can't afford the things on TV
Deep in my heart I abhor you
Can't get food for the kid.

Good God we're gonna rock down to electric avenue
And then we'll take it higher

Who is to blarr.e in what country
Never can get to the one
Dealing in multiplication
And they still can't feel everyone

Out in the streets
Out in the streets
Out in the daytime
Out in the night

Out in the streets
Out in the streets
Out in the playground
In the dark side of town

Oh we're gonna rock down to electric avenue
And then we'll take it higher
Oh we gonna rock down to electric avenue
And then we'll take it higher.

EDDIE GRANT Guyana

LUCINDA RODGERS

G A M B L E R

He lived so recklessly that
His mamma told him, 'Son,
If you never mend your ways
You'll die with your shoes on,
Die with your shoes on.'

He kept on shooting dice
And not once did he pray,
Though seldom was he lucky
He continued anyway.

That he tried with loaded dice
The gamblers had no doubt,
He shook the dice and rolled them,
And then a shot rang out.

He screamed, 'Come take off my shoes,'
Knowing that he would die:
'I wanna make mamma out
a low-down Goddam lie,
Low-down Goddam lie'.

ELMA STUCKEY Black American

Klassical
DUB

dis is a dreadful bad bass bounce
blood a leap an pulse a pounce

riddim cuttin sharp
riddim cuttin sharp
riddim cuttin sharp so

whatta search mi riddim on de hi-fi
whatta dreadful bounce heavy-low
whatta jucky-jucky-jucky-jucky juck-ee

jucky-jucky bounce
jucky-jucky bounce
jucky-jucky bounce

blast an tumble rumblin doun soh!

FIRE FE DE WICKED
venjance on de day
FIRE FE DE WICKED
brimstones in deir bones I say
FIRE FE DE WICKED
blast dem cast dem doun deh

whatta shakeitup drum stick rackle
sharppa dan a, harsha dan a glass-backle riddim
cuttin up a flesh in a I-yah fire fashan
whatta doun soh drop stop bap beat drop

klassikal mystical dub
klassikal mystical dub
klassikal mystical dub

get yu set fe mek yu move out deh!

LUCINDA RODGERS

LINTON KWESI JOHNSON Jamaica/UK

I DON'T TALK TO POP STARS

I don't talk to pop stars
and they don't talk to me
it's a mutual arrangement –
the way we like to be
I don't talk to pop stars
they make me feel depressed
and I won't sit in dressing rooms
and watch them get undressed
I don't talk to pop stars
they really piss me off
I hope they die in poverty
like poor Vincent van Gogh
I don't talk to pop stars
and I hope that you don't too
'cos if you've talked to Billy Bragg
then I won't talk to you
I don't talk to pop stars
won't share their cans of beer
I never nick their underpants
I'd better make that clear
I don't talk to pop stars
I think they should be shot
or gassed, or hung, or sterilised
or the whole bloody lot
I don't talk to pop stars
they really make me sick
especially that Seething Wells
he really is a prick
I don't talk to pop stars
they really make me vomit
I'd rather clean out lavatories
or study Halley's comet
I don't talk to pop stars
I wish they'd go away
and I walk out of pop concerts
when pop stars start to play
I don't talk to pop stars
but listen to my plea –
one day, when I'm a pop star,
will you still talk to me?

ATTILA THE STOCKBROKER UK
'Stockbroker' became part of his stage name
because he worked as a clerk
in a stockbroking firm

Scraping the World away

Every day
I feel like getting on my knees
And scraping the world away.
But what would the people think
If they saw the world disappearing
Into my finger nails?
What is under it all?
A ball of fire?
I think it's the same with people
If you scrape away the bones,
Hatred and blood.
What's left?
Only the kindness of a flower.
But what will happen to the people?
They will get scraped away
Just like the dirt.
But the sky,
How will I scrape that away?
I'll climb a ladder to the top
And pull it all down
But when I've scraped it
Where will I put it all?
Where will I put myself?
I'll lock myself in a cage
And drift away
Or might throw it all in the
BURNING FIRE
and nothing will be left
And I'll start again on another planet.

CLIVE HERBERT WEBSTER
Born UK; mother: Irish, father: Guyanese.
Written at 10

****

A g i e ' s   A d v i c e

You don't have to insist on being yourself.
Never make decisions on the road.
Never put your papers on the table.
And never count your money in the wind.

KEN SMITH UK

A WARNING

If you keep two angels in a cage
They will eat each other to death

ADRIAN MITCHELL UK

THE FAT BLACK WOMAN'S MOTTO ON HER BEDROOM DOOR

GRACE NICHOLS Guyana/UK

It's better to die in the flesh of hope
Than to live in the slimness of despair

SUN
is shining

BOB MARLEY Jamaica

Sun is shining, the weather is sweet
make you want to move, your dancing feet
to the rescue, here I am
want you to know ya, where I stand

When the morning gather the rainbow
want you to know, I am a rainbow too.

To the rescue, Monday morning, here I am
want you to know, Tuesday evening,
just if you can, where I stand

Wednesday morning, tell myself
a new day is rising.
Thursday evening, get on the rise a
new day is dawning
Friday morning, here I am
Saturday evening, want you to know just
want you to know just where I stand

When the morning gathers the rainbow
want you to know, I am a rainbow too
so to the rescue, here I am
want you to know, just if you can
where I stand

We lift our heads and give jah praises
We lift our heads and give jah praises

LO COLE

Sun is shining, the weather is sweet now
make you want to move, your dancing feet
to the rescue, here I am
want you to know, just if you can,
where I, know, know, know, know, where I stand

Monday morning, scoo-be-doop-scoop-scoop
Tuesday evening, scoo-be-doop-scoop-scoop
Wednesday morning, scoo-be-doop-scoop-scoop
Thursday evening, scoo-be-doop-scoop-scoop
Friday morning, scoo-be-doop-scoop-scoop
Saturday evening, scoo-be-doop-scoop-scoop

So to the rescue, to the rescue, to the rescue
awake from your sleep and slumber
today could be your lucky number
sun is shining and the weather is sweet

Life doesn't frighten me

Shadows on the wall
Noises down the hall
Life doesn't frighten me at all
Bad dogs barking loud
Big ghosts in a cloud
Life doesn't frighten me at all.

Mean old Mother Goose
Lions on the loose
They don't frighten me at all
Dragons breathing flame
On my counterpane
That doesn't frighten me at all.

I go boo
Make them shoo
I make fun
Way them run
I won't cry
So they fly
I just smile
They go wild
Life doesn't frighten me at all.

Tough guys in a fight
All alone at night
Life doesn't frighten me at all.
Panthers in the park
Strangers in the dark
No, they don't frighten me at all.

That new classroom where
Boys all pull my hair
(Kissy little girls
With their hair in curls)
They don't frighten me at all.

Don't show me frogs and snakes
And listen for my scream,
If I'm afraid at all
It's only in my dreams.

I've got a magic charm
That I keep up my sleeve,
I can walk the ocean floor
And never have to breathe.

Life doesn't frighten me at all
Not at all
Not at all
Life doesn't frighten me at all.

MAYA ANGELOU Black American

KIDNAP
Poem

ever been kidnapped
by a poet
if i were a poet
i'd kidnap you

put you in my phrases
and meter you to jones beach
or maybe coney island
or maybe just to my house

lyric you in lilacs
dash you in the rain
alliterate the beach
to complement my sea

play the lyre for you
ode you with my love song
anything to win you
wrap you in the red Black green
show you off to mama

yeah if i were
a poet i'd kid
nap you

NIKKI GIOVANNI Black American

poetry patter

Most people ignore most poetry because most poetry ignores most people.

ADRIAN MITCHELL

Short stories were my first serious obsession. Poetry came unexpectedly after I had accepted a girl-friend's invitation to a writers' workshop.

JAMES BERRY

I like writing for people untouched by poetry. I would like them to read poems as naturally as they read the papers, or go to a football match.

MIROSLAV HOLUB

When I was about 10, I discovered the children's library. It saved me.

MEILING JIN

I have a belief that if you don't love something, you'll never be great at it. I made my living as a singer, but I never loved it. But I loved to dance as much as I loved writing.

MAYA ANGELOU

When writing prose, I go straight to the typewriter. With poetry, I work in pencil.

AMRYL JOHNSON

My best ideas for poems come when I'm doing absolutely nothing.

GRACE NICHOLS

* *

Poetry is no longer a tiny minority interest with a tedium factor second to none, but is now considered by many people as a firm base for a great evening out.

ATTILA THE STOCKBROKER

As I am a poet I express what I believe, and I fight against whatever I oppose, in poetry.

JUNE JORDAN

My main inspiration came from the Reggae DJs who pointed the way forward for me. One of the things which I found was that a musical element kept creeping into my poetry because my first love was music.

LINTON KWESI JOHNSON

Sometimes I discover that I'm eavesdropping on myself – I overhear myself mouthing phrases which I then copy down. A poet is perhaps someone who can remain quiet enough to listen to, and notate, the strange, rhythmic voices that are within all of us.

ROGER MCGOUGH

I have got an old, line exercise book with some flower poems in it; sentimental rhyming things which I wrote when I was about eight. I had trouble with rhyme even then . . . I didn't pursue poetry again, until about twenty years later.

MICHELENE WANDOR

index of poets

****

index of first lines

****

acknowledgements

The publishers gratefully acknowledge permission to reprint the following copyright material:

John Agard for 'Spell to Banish a Pimple' and 'Checking Out Me History';
Yansan Agard for 'When'; Jamal Ali for 'The Bum (Calypso)'; Random House Inc. for 'Life Doesn't Frighten Me' from
And Still I Rise Copyright © 1978 by Maya Angelou; Attila the Stockbroker for 'I Don't Talk to Pop Stars'; New
Beacon Books Ltd for 'Flame and Water' from *Lucy's Letters and Loving* by James Berry, published 1982; Bogle-
L'Ouverture Publications Ltd for 'Insec' Lesson' by Valerie Bloom; Jean Binta Breeze for 'Natural High' from *Riddym
Ravings* published by Race Today Publications; Gwendolyn Brooks for 'We Real Cool'; Brother Resistance and Karia
Press for 'Dollar Horror' from *Rapso Explosion*; Maureen Burge for 'Disillusion' from *Ain't I a Woman*, published by
Virago Press 1987; Alison Campbell for 'A Short Note on Schoolgirls'; Basement Arts for 'The Sun Witness' by
Nurunessa Choudhury from *I See Cleopatra*; Century Hutchinson for 'Health Fanatic' by John Cooper Clarke from
Ten Years in an Open Necked Shirt published by Arrow Books 1983; Eunice de Souza for 'Sweet Sixteen'; Tove
Ditlevsen for 'Divorce I' translated by Ann Freeman; Loretta Dumas for 'My Little Boy' by Henry Dumas from *Play
Ebony Play Ivory* published by Random House Inc. 1974; Oxford University Press for 'Touching' from *Latter-Day
Psalms* by Nissim Ezekiel (OUP 1982); John Calder (Publishers) Ltd and Verlag Klaus Wagenbach for 'What
Happens' by Erich Fried translated by Stewart Hood from *100 Poems without a Country* published 1978 by John
Calder (Publishers) Ltd; Nikki Giovanni for 'Kidnap Poem' from *The Black Poets* published by Bantam Books, New
York, 1971; Eddie Grant for 'Electric Avenue'; Savitri Hensman for 'The Cage' from *Flood at the Door* published by
Centerprise Trust Ltd 1979; 'The Teacher' by Miroslav Holub, reprinted by permission of Bloodaxe Books Ltd from
The Fly by Miroslav Holub, translated by Ewald Osers (Bloodaxe Books 1987); Michael Horovitz for 'Enlightenment'
from *Growing Up: Selected Poems and Pictures 1951–79* by Michael Horovitz (Allison and Busby 1979); Accabre
Huntley for 'Me' from *At School Today* published by Bogle L'Ouverture Publications 1977; Mahmood Jamal for
'Objectivity' from *Silence Inside a Gun's Mouth* published by Kala Press 1984; David Higham Associates Ltd for
'Clothes' by Elizabeth Jennings from *The Secret Brother* published by Macmillan; Meiling Jin for 'A Long Overdue
Poem to my Eyes' from *Gifts from my Grandmother* published by Sheba Feminist Publishers; Virago Press Limited for

'Until the Next Time' copyright © Amryl Johnson 1985, published by Virago Press 1985; Bogle L'Ouverture Publications for 'Klassical Dub' from *Dread Beat and Blood* by Linton Kwesi Johnson published 1975 June Jordan for 'Photograph of Managua from Nicaragua Libre' from *Living Room* published by Thunder's Mouth Press Inc, 1985; Jackie Kay for 'Mull'; Deepak Kalha for 'Backsides' and 'Maths' from *Tall Thoughts* published by Basement Writers 1976; Fran Landesman for 'Don't Do It My Way' from *Is It Overcrowded on Heaven* published by Golden Handshake Productions 1981; Miles Davis Landesman for 'Heaven's in the Basement' published by Golden Handshake Productions 1981; Mary Levien for 'Source'; Eddie Linden for 'A Drunken Egotist' from *The City of Razors and Other Poems* published by Jay Landesman 1980; Alonzo Lopez for 'Direction' from *Voices from Wah'kon-Tah* published by International Publishers Inc. 1974; W.W. Norton & Company Inc. for 'Hanging Fire' reprinted from *The Black Unicorn*, Poems by Audre Lorde, copyright © 1978 by Audre Lorde; Aonghas Macneacail for 'i kept on past' which was first published in *Orbis*; Zinzi Mandela for 'If My Right Hand'; Anvil Press Poetry for 'Another Dad' from *Living in Disguise* by E.A. Markham published by Anvil Press Poetry 1986; Leo Songs and Bob Marley for 'Sun is Shining'; A.D. Peters & Co Ltd for 'What the Littlegirl Did' by Roger McGough from *The Mersey Sound* published by Penguin Books Ltd, reprinted by permission of the Peters Fraser & Dunlop Group Ltd; W H Allen & Co for 'Bebe Belinda and Carl Columbus' and 'A Warning' by Adrian Mitchell; Lotte Moos for 'If You Think' from *Time to be Bold* published by Centerprise Trust Ltd 1981; Paul Issa Publications Limited for 'You and Yourself' from *Mutabaruka: The First Poems*; Virago Press Limited for 'A Fat Poem' and 'The Flat Black Woman's Motto On Her Bedroom Door' from *Fat Black Woman's Poems*, copyright © Grace Nichols 1984, published by Virago Press 1984; Grace Nichols for 'Break/Dance'; Marion Boyars Publishers Limited and New Directions for 'Propositions' from *Emergency Poems* by Nicanor Parra published by Marion Boyars Publishers Limited 1977; copyright © 1972 by Nicanor Parra and Miller Williams, copyright © 1972 by New Directions Publishing Corporation; Alvaro Pena-Rojas for 'Green Velvet Suit' from *Men Don't Cry, They Sing*; Kembi Pokereu for 'Dolphins' from *Words of Paradise*: Poetry of Papua New Guinea, published by Unicorn Press; Vasco Popa for 'A Wise Triangle' from *Let's Talk About the Weather* published by Forest Books 1985; Marsha Prescod for 'Women Are Different' from *Land of Rope and Tory* published by Akira Press 1985; Dory Previn for 'did jesus have a baby sister?'; Christopher Cardale (Zolan Quobble) for 'Blue Whale Knowledge'; Artery Media Productions and Chile Cultural Centre for 'Byes' from *Chilean Speech-Chilean Espich* by Mauricio Redoles: a bilingual Spanish/English volume published by Artery Publications and Chile Cultural Centre in the Artery Socialist Poets illustrated series, London 1986. Translated from Spanish by John Lyons; Julie Ridd for 'Toes'; Andre Deutsch Limited for 'I Wake Up' from *Quick Let's Get Out of Here* by Michael Rosen published by Andre Deutsch 1983; Joyce Parkes on behalf of Tadeusz Rozewicz and Mrs Geoffrey Thurley for 'Father' by Tadeusz Rozewicz from *Green Rose* published by John Michael Group of Publishers 1982; Andrew Salkey for 'A Song for England'; Peters Fraser & Dunlop Group Limited and Sterling Lord Literistic, Inc. for 'Young' from *Complete Poems* by Anne Sexton published by Houghton Mifflin 1981, copyright © 1981 by Linda Gray Sexton & Loring Conant, Jr., as executors of the will of Anne Sexton; Kazuko Shiraishi for 'Antelope' from *Seasons of Sacred Lust*; Lemn Sissay for 'The Breath of Death'; 'Agie's Advice' by Ken Smith, reprinted by permission of Bloodaxe Books Ltd from *Terra* by Ken Smith (Bloodaxe Books 1986); Kendell Smith for 'Loneliness'; the family of Michael Smith for 'Ticky Ticky Tuck' from *It A Come* published by Race Today Publications 1986; Forest Books for 'The Lesson' by Marin Sorescu from *Let's Talk About the Weather* published by Forest Books 1985; Carole Stewart for 'I Love You, It's True' from *Watchers and Seekers* published by The Women's Press; Elma Stuckey for 'Gambler' from *The Big Gate* published by Precedent Publishing Inc. 1975; Levi Tafari for 'The Tongue'; Macmillan Publishing Company for 'Mother's Advice to the Bride', Trask translation of the East African poem, reprinted with permission of Macmillan Publishing Company from *The Unwritten Song*, Vol. 1, edited, with translations, by Willard R. Trask. Copyright © 1966 by Willard R. Trask; the family of Vivian Usherwood for 'Loneliness'; Mauricio Venegas for 'Telephone'; W H Allen for 'He-Man' by Michelene Wandor from *Touch Papers*; Clive Herbert Webster for 'Scraping the World Away'; Century Hutchinson Limited for 'The Wherefore and the Why' and 'Inquisitiveness' from *Not to be Taken Seriously* by Colin West; A.P. Watt Ltd on behalf of Michael B. Yeats and Macmillan London Limited for 'The Mermaid' from The Collected Poems of W.B. Yeats; and Benjamin Zephaniah for 'I Love'.

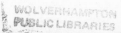